Books by Elizabeth Martina Bishop:

Irish Tinkers
Feathers in the Wind
Canary Portals
My Feet Talk to the Road
Soulmate in a Kayak
Leaping into the Unknown
Malvinia
The Wedding Will Not Take Place
Wind Rushing Through a Nest of Stars
Your Grandmother Knew How To Read Cards
Stonehenge Blues Vol. 1
Stonehenge Blues Vol. 2
Carillon Players and Night Watchmen
The Sleeping Lady of Malta
Floating World
And Then I Heard Them Singing
Round House Dances
The Mud Palace Of Aberdeen
Pavlova Awakening
The Road To Tramore

Elizabeth Martina Bishop, Ph.D.
2675 West State Route 89A, #1100
Sedona, AZ 86336, USA

ISBN-13: 978-1490466736
ISBN-10: 1490466738

BISAC: Poetry / General
Design by Artline Graphics, Sedona.
www.artline-graphics.com

BEACH
SIDE
MOTEL

ELIZABETH MARTINA BISHOP

Table of Contents

PART 1: EVICTION NOTICE

Table of Contents

PART 1

EVICTION NOTICE

Betrayal

We are going to meet at the beach. I know it, I can feel it
So I go to a trendy dress shop,
Filled with the most trendy gypsy clothes
I can imagine. I want to sink my teeth into a new dress because
My lover will be meeting my later this afternoon at four o'clock.
I want to look scintillatingly beautiful for him.

I told the shop owner "I know it, he's gonna propose to me today
After fourteen years of waiting. Haven't you got a red dress?"
She says, don't you know red dresses are for funerals?
What do you want a kimono? I look at her and say,
"Surely the second coming is at hand, I don't see why you have
To be so insulting. Can't you see what it's like to have been waiting
For this man for fourteen years in seven different countries?"
Men are not worth it. you might as well be an African with a spear
Running after an ocelot. Shed it.

Before you were born you shed your skin. Now repeal the apple
In honor of your inner form from which you can never escape.
Repeal the apple to discover your inner core.
Then throw the skin over your head and list your teeth
As the only thing left indigenous to your body.

Now I'm meeting him on the rock.
He's sitting on one rock I'm sitting on another
It wasn't supposed to be like this.
Why won't he look at me in my new dress?

The sand is plush.
But he says I have something to tell you.

I get ready for the proposal.
This is the twenty-fifth in one month.
He says: I want to tell you about my daughter
She got a job at the bank.

Bird Chick Sonnet

Wild bird chick, I want to put you out to pasture
Sooner than later. Even a boatman, oarless and drifting
Would have surrendered, would have let you swim
From beneath the moon into your subterranean room of air.
From my screened porch in Hawaii
I watch as Princess Pele changes her dress of volcanic ash

So many times a day. The volcanic ash rains down
On the skin of the mountain, who knows you as you are
And how you really can be. Does time really exist?
As a scribe of wilderness and fire, the self goes up against the self
In a portrait less probable than air.
Wild bird chick, I want to put you out to pasture.
Galina's squirrels are all sorcerers. They have nibbled
The edges of the Czarina's letters.

Is the hand of fate trying to convince us to square up with debtors?
As wild flying hair will well testify against the logic of the night stars
That belong to the heart forever. What is the vast equation
That will anchor you? There are too many established rules of death
No one has ever known how vast the mirrors are of sleep.
How can you sing into the broken heart of the muse
When the heart is already broken that you choose.

Broken Gourd

When the broken gourd of the sky
began spilling ash
people thought they could enter cockpits
or airplanes and witness everything.

Fly off in a sashay of polite sparks
as if all
that was left in the world to do was just that.

Except that I myself continued to breathe
and overnight help myself
to cream puffs .

Evicted From Property?

How can you be trespassing on your own rented property?

How can you be evicted from that which you do not own?
How can you be evicted for trespassing
On the rights you do not have?
How can a fifteen year old dog, savage an eighty year old woman?

How can an eighty year old woman menace another
If she is crippled, and has a cane?
And song birds live in a cathedral of death,
and husky dogs have abandon their sleds in arctic conundrum

It is better not to answer any questions or to call the dog Miranda
Or to call an elder Miranda or get or have a lie detector test
You must be homeless so get yourself out of this mess
You must be homeless I guess

Perfect Edition

if in a manner of minutes
a small sparrow falls earthward
within a rumor of time's timeless minutes
what happens to us all?
we are disinterested
and yet we are affected

that is the teaching
of those not yet
dejected or forewarned
about the exclusionary rights
of the forgiven
who have trespassed with their own bodies
being here on earth and not somewhere else
as what was planned by divinity forestalling

if in a matter of minutes a small sparrow falls
earthward in a rumor of time's timeless minutes
who ushers in timeless ghosts of time
who ushered in a manner of minutes

when time runs out of time
no one knows precisely how many angels
dance on the head of a pin without detention
no one knows how many angels confess their jiggory pokery
on the head of a pin
then at night when thieves break in
and begin in earnest their soul-mockery
then ravens begin to float in earnest
on heaven's cloud terraces
leaving no trace of where they have ever been

at Skid Row at night when thieves begin working miracles
it makes you think of what you did before
you dropped your body and slid into the cosmic dance
of ocean floor and sky-roof
it makes you think of what you did
before you ever thought of dropping the body
if hidden in wind-driven clouds and theatrical
castles and palaces

if among cloud-ridden steeples
a half dead sparrow truly dead his life incomplete
and yet completed
whatsoever person hears the word of god
what is up with that
was anything ever heard
as it was in the beginning
whatever happened, never breathe a word
of what you know to anyone
they will put you in the lunatic asylum again I know they will

if a dead sparrow truly dead, grief-stricken
at once the relatives will begin to borrow
rumors of other persons half living or half alive
who occupy the nethermost regions of the air
knows how near the end he was

would he not have rented furniture and moved
out of the bedroom into the living room
where everyone could spot him
the pantomime of air is filled with leaves
almost turning in their bus passes
and their sheriff badges
do you think he really believed
in jesus and the angels or in something else
that kept him going the god-self chronicled in the same way.

Dream of a Mansion

I

I am a wealthy woman living in a mansion
With two children

II

My husband is a wealthy Hispanic man
He wears the most up-to-date ties and clothes
He wants to read the New York Times
All over the house.

III

I go to his rich parents' house
And bring my two girls.

IV

The husband asks what's the matter.

V

I say to my husband, "Never Again!"
And throw him out in the street.

VI

This dream is part of a longer dream
Featuring Jackie Chan.
In a wheelchair, I move my two children around,
At the end of the dream a black man
Pushes my children in a wheelchair.

VII

Jay Lenno, Jack Benny and other nighttime
Comedians discuss my dream.

Dream Sequence

1. Back in the mansion my husband is enjoying the company
    Of tailors. Jewish people who own the mansion.
2. This particular group of people have chosen to be participants
    in a mansion experiment
3. How will living in the mansion affect everyone? Are there inner
    secret rooms that are not completely furnished? What about the
    afterlife?
4. I enter one of the rooms and I notice this is a leaderless group,
    but several leaders are women.
5. One of the group leaders goes to another room in the mansion
    and writes a song on the other side for a friend.
6. I notice all the friends are pleasant. And even though this may
    be the afterlife, no one is going through a purgatorial
    experience.
7. I buy a bicycle and ride inside and outside. The bicycle is a
    vehicle for transformation, it seems.
8. The bathroom sings. This is not my dream. The toilet seats are
    clean. Everything in the bathroom is kept pretty nicely. It's like a
    scene from the thirties. Well, they're not that perfect.
9. All the rooms in the mansion are clean and pleasant and very
    luxurious and at a higher golf club level than that I'm used to
    leaving in.
10. I meet an old man who likes me very much.
11. I sew a beautiful gauze dress that's the color of green jade. It is
    silky beautiful gauze dress for my therapist. This is not my
    dream.
12. I'm weaving little strands. This time I sew smocking on a dress.
13. I've seen more rooms in the mansion. I ask the leader of the
    group if I could see the secret rooms that are held under wraps

that are not open to all the visitors. What I'm saying is I'm looking at the facade of life and now I am looking past the facade. And now I'm looking at this man that I was attracted to and planning for a life that's behind the facade.

14. There was a ledge to be a pile of beautiful ballgowns and fabric. Things I knew women in the women's group would like.

15. Two women from the women's group who are Jewish tailors lead us to their secret rooms where they make their clothes.

16. All the rooms in the house are pretty clean and dull except for the Jewish women taylor's rooms, which had an air of the secret sacred feminine about them.

17. I'm very glad for my new part, I'm grateful I'm glad that I'm cleaning the room.

18. We're all anxious about parking and getting a new art experience.

19. I meet an old man. He's short, fat squat bald and dull. We embrace as if we're in a bordello. I tell him that he's totally the most unattractive person I've ever seen in my life.

20. Can we be married next life and can we find a good place like this mansion to be in, perhaps tiny but full of consciousness, but perhaps in the next life the place of consciousness will be clean and we'll be friends.

Memory of a Dead Sparrow

Don't wash your dirty linen in the park
In all the secret places of the heart, let the fire burn itself out
It is I am innocence who would ask what is with this poem?
Also know this the sparrow lives in a dark underbrush,
In a dark place where no one knows him
He is anonymous as the lost blood
Of other winters. You figure that one out.
The ghost of Aunt Martha time does not matter here.
If in s manner of minutes a small sparrow falls earthward
In time-honored rumors of minutes assail him with the truth
No one knows exactly how many angels confess
Their jiggory-pokery on the head of a pin.
If at night, when on skid row, thieves begin their miracles
It makes you think of what you did before you dropped the body.
Among wind-driven rooms of stone castles and palaces
No one knows what you have gone through
Nor do they want to know, really they don't
How did the sparrow figure out
The end of the world really near at hand?
Grief-stricken, did his relatives tell him
Or some other infinite source he missed
Nor did anyone ever understand
What needed to be understood
As fully as it was deemed it should.

In a matter of minutes when a small sparrow falls earthward
Who when felled unexpectedly, who sheds a tear
In the choir stalls unexpectedly no one makes amend
After the funeral is ended and everyone goes forth in peace
Or maybe they don't remember any details about the legacy

Of that person's august life. At my mother's funerals
My father told me stay by my side don't say a word
Momma is not going to buy you a mocking bird in fact
She won't leave you a single necklace or any jewels
To bedeck your miserable body with since you
Gave up dancing you're so out of shape it's not funny
Well dad if you did not worship the family dog
More than me and take care of her more carefully
What happened would never have happened to me
Or to you for that matter in fact you almost gave your life
For your son and what did he care did he end up
Loving you all the same or did he suddenly
Take up the palette a ghost of time's restless
Minutes who will save you really no one will
There is really no one like you and you know it
Whatever happens everyone will know it
Before it ever happens anyway people are becoming
So psychic these days they scarcely know how to
Complete a memory map of the entire world
Or complete washing their dirty linen in public

And become a first rate artist?
Dad all you have to do is pick up the phone
And call me but instead you want to suffer
And act as if it is still 1943 and I am still at home
With mum and you don't even want to get to know me
Or you didn't have the time in a strange way I still love you
Yes I do dad

Grief-stricken did he know how near the end he was or not
Perhaps a sparrow floats out to see as listless as a mother
Who asks that all the furniture be moved from her room
And that her bed be put by an open window in the living room
Where all can catch a glimpse of her at the last minutes
Of her incarnation? Do you think the sparrow
Believes in anything but the supreme goddess
Who puts before you the beginning and end of sewing sessions,

Coffee klatsches movie get-togethers or having tennis lessons
Or bowling matches before the end is near?
How entertain the ghosts of wayward stations
How maintain your composure and your proper
His multiple timelines are so all encompassing
He doesn't have to reincarnate alone
When the thunderous applause happens
Always a lightening flash fails and misses its mark completely
Once again you are alone
And anything that happens fails to strike home.

How many artists leave their easels in the park?
Suddenly everyone is willing to blurt out the evening new
The impudent speaks unwisely about the wise
And the wise make mistakes and grapple with the truth
Even so you are branded a liar even if you are truthful
And wander around the hedgerow with a bible
Or a blank piece of paper. A pen? Something must be
Going on knitting needles continue knitting
Even after dark why should I have to defend myself to you?
A skylark knows better how to jump off a roof
Or into a swimming pool some kind of shenanigans
The archer misses the bull's eye all the time.
What of it?

How many artists leave their easels in the park?
Suddenly everyone is willing to blurt out the truth
The stock market crash as well as Mother Shipton's Prophecy
Are totally out of date. Nostradamus?
Oh everyone has had enough of him.
The channel is broken that was once open.
So what if everyone stores data in computers
And decides to leave it all behind.
The diner the little walks to the station
The price of eggs too much to comment upon
They will shut down all the super-markets
After the grand slam tennis final

Suddenly the veins in your hands have grown
Almost unrecognizable and your voice is lowered almost in a whisper
And nothing sounds the same
The words recited are a little under sung
By the multitude who have to listen to your fol de rol
Oh, but, come on, my dear, don't go spoiling your life work
Come on in out of the rain before the song begins again.

Know when to come in out of the rain my dear
Know which side of the toast is buttered
It just a matter of time when everyone will be afraid
And they won't know where to move to
Why spoil the makings of your life work?
Come now come along inside bring your umbrella inside
Why not volunteer at a prison?
By Monday or Tuesday fellow workers
Or colleagues begin their wisecracks about inclement weather
The price of gimcrackers eggs dog walkers
Begin their alphabets of city-streets
Book-seller open their awnings
Once again everyone realizes life is sweet
Among the nomadic artists.
Nothing so reprehensible as the life of the damned
Or the man that runs a stoplight on a city street
Forewarned without warning
I wonder how many parishioners are content
Have their attended church even once
Before the new minister came
You know the one who features the choirmaster
And speaks out of both sides of his mouth
The cost of canvases and colored chalks are out of sight
The price of birth baths impossible to decipher

Today haven't you discerned what happens to everyone
When each person and his brother vies with one another
To do more than his share at what cost to mother earth
And to the health of rivers

When worker drops his body hasn't it become quite clear
Who is adept at giving dalliance to time-honored truths?
The grand slam poetry contest is on once again
No matter that it takers beer to even begin the round
Is it any wonder like it or not
Such soul painting conceived in madness
Of minarets and mosques often find their way
To the auction block where the artists are tied for first place?
Is it any wonder then faithfully rendered
In the Marketplace anything is up for grabs?

Each soulful rendition of a painting
Sighing men wipe each other's eye
As time demands to know who is adept
At such bitter dalliance with time shared
And god given truths spawns a lesser truth
Than what can be countered with what is
Tied for first place at the auction block?
This happens not out of ignorance

But rather in a momentary embrace
Of a blameless dance of truth and justice
A momentary dance blames and innocent
In the first instance at first almost everyone looks in denial
Innocent or involved with other things
Self-absorbed but I am innocent of any wrong doing
What are you doing?
Someone suspects no one could be innocent
Of some kind of wrongdoing.

Under duress, is that true you succumbed to the temptation
Of how many confessions heard an unheard?
Tweezers can uproot the last whisker of a beard
And in the end hair-splitting decisions
Are those that are made at births, weddings, wakes, and in between
When nothing is really going on, today don't you know
You must puzzle over the memory of ministering angels?

The Give Away

What I have here are poems egrets herons, moons, broadback swans,
Birds that never proved anything except by flying,
Pavlova in the Ivy House,
A masquerade of feathers poised
What did she learn from swans?
Except the same thing everybody learns
That the body burns as easily as ash, turning and returning
What I have to give you are poems for anyone and everyone
Who will listen
And even for those who do not want to listen
Those listeners who are deaf to the word
And dumb to the touch of words
As the hummingbird brushes past the cheek of winter
The blue lips of the snow maiden turn cold
She is dead to herself and to the world.
She sleeps on a pillow that is stone.
An eagle stole her heart.
What I have for you are poems.
Love poems, spoken, whispered, half-told stories
Half-harvested, detours, angles, turns in the road,
Stories woven by wrens, robins, popinjays magpies,
Woodpeckers, bobwhites, flickers,
And even sung in choruses by less courageous birds.

In the dance beneath the pookas' blameless
Hooves, an undertow,
A malingering, as well as the lisping words of nature,
The voice of Magdalena telling me, never go back,
Never return to the nectared cave in Tibet,
In Basra, in Alexandria," where I have stayed for centuries.

Emptiness, fullness, emptiness, what is sauce for the goose,
Is always best for the gander
In the Gypsy ovens in Treblinka, where life was offered up
It cost us nothing but our shawls, our words our wishes, our sashes,
To ducker with a dying woman, to ducker with a dying swan,
Her house covered with ivy,
Who stands on the threshold of life playing with Tarot cards?

When the breath of life belonged to the frail bones of a physician,
It's just like the wishbone of a hawk or a goose, and eagle or a hare,
When the breath departs
Only a hairbreadth of distance between moon and moon,
Bridges the distance.

I cannot go home until I recall every last thing in my life.
The plunge into Wash Pond, Long pond, Round Pond,
An abandoned marriage at the lip of a sliver of life
Called the River. Called the riverbed of song.
Unburdened with these memories, my breadbasket is full.
Empty, full
Absence and presence, honor, honor song.
Upholding the elders' presence
The coverlet of uneasy stars
I remember Mariel
She wore a white dress
She gave sermons from a pulpit not her own in a church
That was a stone to a large amethyst stone
A stone so large that you could sit around it all day
And never feel alone.

Magpies used to gather around her house at quail Run,
Where her husband held folk dancing workshops.
He was Slavic, Czechoslovakian, he never tired of teaching
Mariel told him she was ill, but he did not believe her.
While cancer danced around her, around the quilt of her existence
She recalled a trip in London to Jenny's house
Blind Jenny knew her records,

Told her the exact moment of her death,
Mariel wore white, had been an opera singer from Pennsylvania,
She never varied from her role.

Each day she picked a different opera.
In the amethyst studded church she brought out her
Begging basket from her Assiniboine rooted genealogy
Reverend Horse watched, fingering his bowtie nervously,
As she gave her last sermon for Valentine's Day.
She told of a great hawk that came to watch her at quail run
Perched on her tiny bird house with eyes that never fled from her
Soul's reckoning.

While she unpinned the feathers of the story
Everyone in the congregation wept
And the minister's wife made clear that angels everywhere
Were blowing trumpets
Next Sunday the epitaph she gave was brief as a symbol
Sounding in an empty wind.
The idea of death danced before each person in the room
While the portraits of grand masters paled
As the last tree growing was felled by a scythe of light.

Green Tara Poem

The only altar worth having is the Green Tara

Beneath a green umbrella of interwoven leaves
no other goddess, please,

no other deity I mean
and yet
dozens of peacock feathers
spreading throughout the galaxy

I know the soul
is trying to decide
whether to come back again
as a sunflower or as a small melon
as a codfish on a string or as a selkie
the kind of one that has swallowed five golden rings
according to the myth reviled
in the reverberating tones of a selfless thunder being

Sherman Alexie, my hero, perhaps he alone has the literary answer
as well as the rest of the tribal people on or off the rez
each one of them collectively knows
what is what and who it is who discovered America.

my car arrests itself at stop lights because it knows does not exist
but it refused to be stopped by something else
not worth thinking about
did you say the Chinese or the Norwegians
discovered america

ah friend that you would not understand
eclectic moves of the piano player
who has been playing ragas at the Brewery
for years that affair with the jazz pianist
ah friend that was a real tug of war
a-push-me-pull-you if there ever was one
what a clown, all part of my past life
of which I am no longer a true part.

By Invitation Only

who was really invited, the Indians?

I was invited to a kind of ice cream social event
as these kind of get together get ups seem to go,
nothing seemed out of the ordinary, no, not so,
The notice seem to read in plain English
on that sacred wall at Crystal Magic:
you know how such things are in Sedona,–
the notice stated the need for keeping good company:
Hafiz for breakfast on Sunday!
with my companion in tow, wow.
I muscle-tested my response,
ow, you almost hurt my shoulder.
and, as vibes go golden doors opened and closed
listen, I want a straight answer from one of my spirit guides
so I read and reread the notice that reads: yes, you all are invited
young and old alike, fat and thin, whatever you like come as you are
we can nibble on cranberries, raisins, or pomegranates
or I can go ahead and cook some artichokes and yams
since I have home-grown gardens in the outback.
after all, how sacred is Mother Earth's Planet?

when a caretaker appeared on the stairway
wearing red, for heaven's sake, I put to him:
can't you choose a different color, mate?

he said; I used to live here in this state you know
that's going back few years
but what can you do
everything I say is true

did you know the only property
george washington willed his son
was graciously selected by him as he was crossing the Delaware
that a sacred journey is depicted on a china plate
sold of late at American Fairs for fifty-two dollars and thirty cents.

in doing that particular dance of wayward circumstance
my spirit guide announced old lady died
right over here on these porch steps
one minute before you came
must have been coming to her
whatever it was, a heart attack
just a few days ago I hadn't a clue
she ever needed assistance
until she dropped dead like a mocking bird
on the front lawn, right while
was eating breakfast: one two three
just like that for christ's sweet sake
that got everyone annoyed
no one would dare interrupt a ritual passing
is that a fact, I asked, perhaps
in making that statement
I could be called some kind of good
neighbor even to myself, I suppose
because if I'm here, I am really present
not just for the asking not just for the taking
but rather enacting surreal multiple cases
of semi-forgiven cases of mistaken identity

to partake of a breakfast in a stranger's house
now that would be something else, but
where's the beef and where's the porridge
all they seem to have on hand are hazel nuts and raisins
I'd rather prefer a few chucked off ears of corn
to do the Indian elders proud some bit of good
for the length of the journey undertaken
to get up those rickety front porch steps

at nine o'clock in the morning
guests seemed to have run out of sleeping bags
on the first quatrain wine became almost invisible
and was offered up as a blessing

between druidic bardic sessions an unemployed radio announcer
shouted the credits: now we're entering the spirit of the bardo
I could do with a cuppa of tea just like in England
but there's no cuppa tea around here

since I've been on vacation
I fear I might have been had this once
suddenly a music therapist went into high gear
and struck a brass gong with a velveteen mallet
I'm an adjunct faculty in the psychology department

in case you feel affronted by inter-tribal rivalries
or the size of the psychology faculty, suddenly,
she offered up an Indian bonnet from an old Sioux indian
she had known. I don't know who raided the grave exactly

but my spirit guides told me try this thing on and ever since
and somehow it stuck on my head and I have felt honored at least
but still at this gathering they have no more chairs
people kept crying out for more popcorn and hazelnuts
and raisins
roasted partridge and squab:
they must've thought they were at Oxford
or at Ascot where American Indians never ever entered the picture
what kind of mystery play was this? I wondered.

suddenly in what was supposed to be an elegant down home breakfast
the leader intoned a quatrain that sounded
suspiciously like some kind of rain dance
or white buffalo woman's gavotte
the leader of the group, Danielle, likened her gavotte to an Irish stew
playing a tiny drum or tambourine, I forget which,

she took out an umbrella
she is here, she is here, she said: eagle man or
eagle woman, either one of them will do
are all right with me:
they are here and she is here and we are here too
wearing an incredible white buckskin outfit,
she is here, she is here she is here at last
let's all shed a tear for the poor Indian dear
where does that leave me, I wondered. I must be an outcaste too.

suddenly there was a gnashing of teeth in the gallery
now the music therapist made an intervention
she stood by the door and hit a brass gong very quietly
all thirteen poets could have been be laid out on a gurney
to have recreational therapy or tete a tete meetings

Danielle said to the music therapist,
can you add anything to this
radiant ceremony-bearer of feathers in the wind?
what could the music therapist do
but play more music on her gong
and twirl innocently in her sarong?

wait a minute! I asked Danielle the all time gracious hostess
what about that poster on the wall? it
advertized dance, an inter-tribal event,
not at all just like breakfast and poetry
breakfast and poetry, where are the dancers?
Instead' I notice after hearing all the poetry
the poets are laid out, why aren't they
dancing in ecstasy? Who stole the lock from the hen-house door
is what I want to know and why did the realtor association
permit this invasion from those posing as non-indians
I don't want anyone walking out this room laughing

whoever lied about the happening on the poster
should have known better

then to assail the wits of Sister Coyote

Moral:

This was an incredible learning experience produced by white buffalo calf woman and her veritable minions and associates of associates

Heartbeats

When I say
my heartbeats
for you I really mean it

until it doesn't anymore
what I mean is
what I mean by this
is a man studying in a healing temple

I would be embarrassed to hear what happened next
I would block my ears with sand
if I knew what would happen next

they try to analyze this
while ambrosia pours out from her ears
and the lion sleeping beside Giza
unfolding his paws is raw with sandstone thorns

perhaps you are having me on, Cassandra,
because the man in the healing temple,
the woman in the healing temple
what were they really saying to us?
were they trying to communicate loving thoughts
we just couldn't quite pick up
because you know sometimes
even the most precious
grandmother's radar is sometimes off

and when the teacher died
the student gazed lovingly out at sea

heard the music of the spheres
spilling from the innards of the moon-driven tide
and of course suddenly the student knew there was no death
and breathed his spirit lout of him
as one night his old teacher walked into him
he'd find himself unable to look away

suddenly his gaze healed millions
it's just that he came from the wrong country
and the wrong disciple smiled at him.

Holocaust Allusions

The last I heard

the first dream consisted
of a silver sugar bowl,
a family heirloom of sorts,
it used to sit right over there on the lazy susan
next to marigolds the color of marmalade and amber

I want to write my grandmother a letter
she used to tell me: we try so hard
to understand her poetry, but we simply can't

grandmother,
it's not worth it,
don't bother
you do enough
for everyone else
but you've left someone out
it's about my daughter

you never tried her picture out
next to my eldest, the one born
to a bloody Englishman,
god forgive him

later in the dream when I looked
at the sugar bowl, I never suspected
it was brimming with sacred ash
ash that came from Louisiana
or the old Ohio or even the Mississippi

oh only say that you'll be mine
and in no other's arms entwine

it's about Indian names all right
a woman run a marathon in pink tights
and a black t-shirt that reads
my-Indian-name-is-runs-for-beer

when she spits at my daughter's back
I remember my grandmother's vanity table
don't look back, the past is almost over
flood with unbelievable memories
dead center there is nothing left
to mourn

now I want to return to the dream
six foot under in a tomb enclosure
meant for kings or queens or servants

what's written on the marble slab
in Roman numerals may signify
the monkey god or maybe his cousin
depending on mass consciousness
anything you want

depending on the level of the dreamer
gone to heaven or gone out to lunch
I don't which
I have an astrological hunch
two or eleven can mean
the same thing
in the eyeless midnight of the dream

I am a banner of a dream
draped over my left shoulder

I'm not sure if the feast
of the twelve grandmothers
keeps god alive or not
or whether Creator or Great Spirit
has a bounty on its head

you, my daughter plays an uneasy violin
before you go away I reach for the soap
dish one last time
just fiddling around
is what the news reporter says

because you are different
you have to be the best in town
true, the sheriff always kept
his eagle eye on you

a thousand parchment skins
could never be placed on recall
in pitch and putt games
with the soap dish

who would have thought the sugar bowl
awoke the memory of the children from the past
children who ran so fast
while sugar granules slid underfoot
like coal cinders in winter or like sand in summer heat

if anyone ever imagined of falling down
they knew they could be shot
who knew how to move away
in time for crystal night to take effect
it was all part of history
so the people say

why live in denial

when a Polish gentleman
is arrested in another town
in Ohio but not in Germany
auto-unions could interfere
but is it fair to extradite the clown
perhaps one leaves it up to family

in that way a heart transplant
may
take him
out of tombstone
with great finality

The Emergence of a Sacred Sign

Rosalie attended a workshop on subliminal healing. It included
The notion of how to interpret sacred signs. The workshop
Took place on Monday afternoon after the poetry reading Society
Was held by Friends of the Library and before the Neighborhood
Association for the Prevention of Cruelty to Animals met
To discuss leash laws & getting your pet spayed and such like.

The issue of sacred signs, what did it mean? Rosalie wondered
As she struggled to interpret the zebra crossings and decode
The ravens congealing on the horizon. after her morning coffee.

One night after the workshop Rosalie dreamed and dreamed.
Angels flew out of the floor and out of the ceiling.
She was baffled and astonished by the strange light
Emanating out of the tasseled Persian rug.
An angel named Hank said he was her brother.
An angel named Myrtle played The Blue Danube
And the invisible keys of a piano moved and suddenly wend dead.
And Rosalie was sold by the parrot-headed can
Hank appeared to tap along the floor. Dreams were a sign
Of the angels parading in a spiritual garden of deceased spirits.

Now she lay alone in her bed as she awoke next morning
And began decoding the maple leaf pattern on the wall.
She opened the window drapes and began to sob. Light she said.
This too is a sign. Parting the blinds is as much a sign as love
Pirouetting like a hawk across the shuddered dark of sleep.

The Art of Swimming

We had never met at any time before,
Yet, hidden behind my shoulder,
You were standing, watching over,

Preparing to open a camera shutter,
Aiming a camera at my retina.

Widening its vast expanse,
As my pupil went on swimming,
Into a field of shimmering stars,

Already flying overhead did birds
Seize the moment to soar heavenward?

At least, the way I recall the story,
The place where I was standing,
Was Broadway and Fourteenth.
Looking svelte in my new black boots,
Wearing my new suede tan mini-skirt,

As I was standing there, doing nothing,
Perhaps I was thinking of what would happen.
Or, of doing nothing later during the day.
I may have wondered what impact this memory would have
On my digestion, and the connective threads of my tubal ligature.

Last Saturday, I recall
While I was looking at the models in the shop window.
Somehow I knew for sure for whom the bullet was meant:
My soul. And yet, I could not die, that was impossible.

Although the effect of death
Was instantaneous,
I found myself gasping for air,

Isn't there a scholar somewhere who lives
This side of Killaloe or County Kildare?
Who could make a rather fascinating
Scientific discovery? I mean about death
And how upon one's death, one is not
Really so aware as all that.

Still wondering what would happen next,
In the next moment I witnessed
Tiny specks of light, magnolia
Blossoming and unfolding in watery threads.

Footsteps, creeping up
Up behind me ever so slowly,
Wave upon wave,

Deafening with a sweet music,
The light thickening its contour,
In darkened silhouette,
Rounded shapes angling into brightness,
A green shade fading into darkness.

Until you opened
The petals of a flower,
Veiled, closed, pressed,
I didn't see the makings of a prism, a rainbow.
Imprisoned within a jar,
Pupa eyes pressed up

Against a heavy-lidded earth,
Enfolded within a nest,
A casket of tiny limbs,
Swimming in filigreed threads,
Impervious to light's flickering
Impermanence.

Could I have known,
This trapdoor swinging open,
Where it would lead,
Leading to an inner sacred spring,
Bubbling outwardly,
Earth's treasure unburied,
The cave of a little flower,
Quickening with the voice
Of ancient stones uncovered?

For this is how it was.
At the moment of my death,
It seemed you taught me
The art of swimming.

In a life of exile,
You held my heart,
My mind spinning wildly,
My heart dancing
In counterfeit waves,
Brimming with love,
This ecstasy spilling
Beyond boundary.
I was no longer a slave.

Dowsing for "The Star" Tarot Card

What difference does it make
A soothsayer lowered
A tin bucket for well-water,
And brought it up eye-level
For all to catch sight of
At a widow's wake?
Who thought that an irreverent gesture
For careless wind-drinkers, sky-walkers,
For gamblers and poachers?

Everyone knows the boat in the picture
Has already tipped over.
Bobcats, quail
And beaver have already
Found winter quarters.

Whatever has happened,
Has already happened.
Been asked to move on
From Skibbereen to Rathfarnham,
We never looked back.

On glittering jewels
Beneath pale surfaces
That wound us as we drown.
In the bright blue water
Of a dream,
What horse throws off its rider?

Yet, jewels still glimmer
Beneath surfaces.
Of the blue, shimmering water.
O waking dream,
If only you knew the difference
Lying in the green mirror
Maybe someone else's lost
Chances are your own.

Do you really think
The parched lips of the hungry ghost
Will bend down to drink? A person
Thirsting for what was meant or what is not
May not be forgotten

How long must I wait?
At four, I wake in and stretch my legs.
Yapping before the moon, coyote dogs…
Doorways are closed
That might have been left open.

Distracted by the weather,
The voices of small crickets
Lean from grass cages
Besides saffron blossoms
In moon-drenched cairns,
People are afraid to recite fables
Of their past lives to lovers.

Tell me again your half-story.
What can I tell you about my life
Without deceiving you further?
How blind I was.
I didn't understand
The final words
For family genealogy.

Watches tick on the wrist of the wind.
When the motor-making light
Will have finished with the dark,
Birds with wicker wings will sing,
Will sing the famine of the heart.

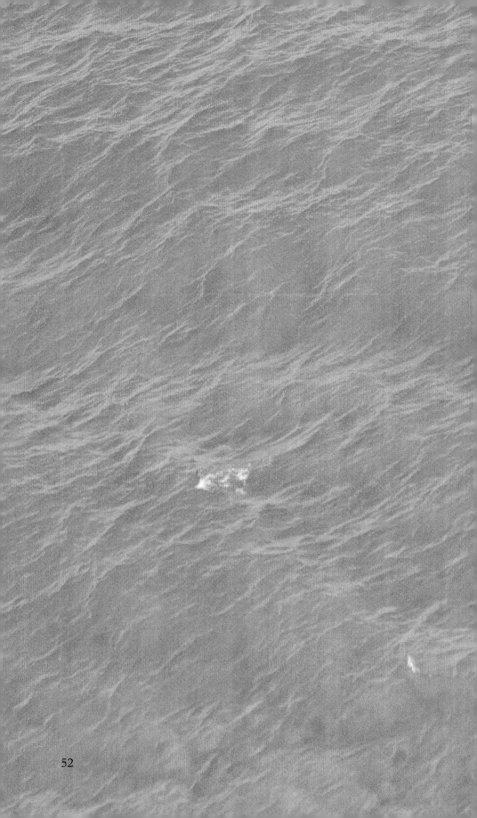

PART 2

SAMUEL'S
BREAKFAST

Hymn to Grief

Come minstrels, with harp and tambourine
Come travelers, come money-making buskers,
From evergreen glades in Saskatoon.
Come troubadours with Yamahas.

Be greedy for healing
As leaf to leaf converses with the wind
Know what to tell your angel
When your angel takes you to task,
You've got to know how to answer
At that particular moment when she asks,
"So what's the deal here on earth," you tell her
"I have so much to live for,"
But overhearing this conversation,
Your friend hasn't the same answer
Have I dialed the wrong number?
I hear Margery tell the angel over and over

She wants to throw herself
In front of a car, a bus, or a train.
In that order? I tell her instead
Consider the possibility
Of life after death.
Consider the body, the life of the spirit
As multi-dimensional,
Life's waking breath.
I hired a circus troupe of charlatans,
Barkers, bankers, ventriloqual artists.
I hired tight-rope walkers, dwarfs, gymnasts,

Giant trapeze acrobats, imposters, acrobatic-aerobic champions
My friend listened to what they said.
About the nature about the nature of free will and determinism

Then speaking to her in a voice
Above a whisper I told her
The voice of spirit is holy.
Life is as good as the perfume of
Gladiolas, petunias, zinnias, and begonias.

I begged her, take a second look
Corncrakes, rooks in the field
They know there is so much to live for.

Look at the orchard,
Full of Darwinian Buddhas.
The orchards will tell you,
Go ahead, climb that hill.
By tomorrow, perhaps she will

It's not that I didn't tell her
Half a dozen times over dinner,
Over picnic lunches
Beside samovars,
Beneath trellised arbors in peaceful meadows
In subterranean terraced gardens,
Lined with wisteria, honeysuckle, trumpet vine,
On porticos, besides pools, ponds, and lakes,
Near verandahs, in half-sunken ships,
On subways, on mountain tops, in wind-filled corridors
Beside tranquil pools,
What do you want to be inscrutable for, Margery?

Life is not puffed up nor jealous.
The body is no match for mind
And spirit. There is no separation
Of church and state. Scribes,

Persians, Greeks, and Chaldeans, all are only human,
Their bubble pipes break
The same as in Lebanon
As anywhere else

From Tashkent comes the sound
Of the drum, the kangling trumpet; the one
Carved from a thigh bone of my aunt's grandfather.
I now know blue sheep do not run from man when driven.
Yet, still it remains a puzzle how to hush a waking child.

I wonder what the snow leopard is feasting on
Beside the cairn of impossible stones, what does he see?
Has there been a report of an accident?
Some report of love being set aside?
Is it vehicular homicide? Torn from the skin of an embered fire
Why sparks leap while love cringes?
Within the glad green feast of tall grass,
What can be said of one who abandons another? Invite them
Both knight and hermit take a bow, one after the other.

In the Spirit of Mindfulness

As compassionate Mother
And doctor to the tarnished flesh of souls,
Blessing wayward pilgrims on the road,
Where are they the lost seekers of your word?

Dropping faded fruit
In embrace of earthly entanglement,
Fruit bruises all too easily,
As it paints itself in unearthly colors.
Unless plucked by the chill hand of winter,

Moving in the wake of rivers,
Hushing, brimming with mindfulness,
Motionless in her surround,
The jeweled stars of Mother Earth
Will not refuse to dance.
In the embrace of her presence.

Empowered by the beating of your dancing heart,
Releasing humanity from the chains of impermanence,
In walking, sitting, or standing meditation,
Knowing full well the sacred manner of your love,
Sorrowful, let me not swim into an ocean of fear.

No more filled with anger of small-minded defeats,
No more longing for lean arrows of half-finished dreams,
Nor for a platform built upon deceit's premise
Whose are these self-limiting mind sequences, and patterns
Allowing me to stumble like a blind person.

Unless shuttered in a prison of darkness, grief-stricken,
Let me no more be exiled by the emptiness of words.
Witnessing the harmony of your threaded covenant,
No more felled by the thorns of impious speech,
O Mother Earth, let me live more and more in a steadfast way.

O Amma, more Holy than Changing Woman
And all the followers of the Holy People,
Igniting a sand painting of a thousand colors,
Outpouring Nightway Chants sung within
The regions of the Four Sacred Mountains,
At dawn, luminous and calm, you stand before all Creation's home.

Moment by moment, the land is embraced
In a shimmering expanse of a greater goodness gained.
Refusing to sing, tongueless, would a linnet cry?
Breathing, would a dust mote inhale a road?
Would breath refuse a sieve of words?
Would mask untie its feathered hymn from clouds?

Before Monster Slayer and the Twins?
When hurled on your path, unasked,
Dropping a fragrant wind, would a rose petal
Wither and decay? Sighing, would a pine tree widen
Wind-filled aisles to include a narrow music's logical reprieve?

In a granary of gold, in the practice of almsgiving,
Would beggars drop their begging bowls
Removing their spiritual coats, bowing before dying?
Refusing to honor the stopped breath of the pilgrim,
Overturning a tureen of stars, would a heathen

Dare to chant a threnody? Felling a temple of prayer,

Detained, exiled in truth's lair of nothingness,
Would all purveyors of formless symbols (of Nirvana)
Cease spinning their dharma threads and sing?

Park silken wing, part canticle of truth,
Opening a purse of sacred fire,
Subtracting wrinkled wings,
Can a milkweed pod, eyeless,
Fly its tented gods forever into sky?
If not, who steers a visionary to rooms of stone?

How does spirit instill the will to grasp
Absence or presence of mind still matters,
Brimming with fragile, greening cells
Whirling, do leaves dissolve
Close stems in amens and salaams?
Mapped within heaven's heart,
The milk of what is human
Also holds loving kindness.

Looking a Gift Horse in the Mouth: Tarot Recipes

Hanging on withies curved and rounded
Under sagging tent canvas, rain-sodden and gray
A client poses a question to the old hag within
              This is a question posed to many readers
Well traveled by headless horsemen and Robert Johnson
The great blues guitarist from a long time ago.

How does a woman know whether she draws the right card?
So, singing at midnight, she may ask herself
Drawing that bright mythic water from a well,
If truly holy, would I sense it?
Would I know the source?
Had it been contaminated by deer poachers, by lepers,
By thieves running blindly in the spare
Quarters of the lonely and maimed.

If I draw past-life parallels from a holy well
If I draw past-life lessons and parables
Will I know whether the holy water will quench my thirst?
Will I know if my child carries the correct chromosomes
If I ride a horse will the pooka take me,
Offset the Tower card on a detour past my destiny
Under the moon-drenched shadow of a one-horse town.

Will the horse sell at auction?
Will I dislike the bride price?
Since my mother always said:
Never on any account, speak ill of others.

Since it's best not to be disagreeable,
Sign the consent form with a smile.
Look at the canary in the cage,
Be available, warble, sing, poet sing.

Now that I know it may be possible
To unlock the fear of making old bones
Scholars and airline stewardesses alike have always told me,
Don't overshoot the runway while playing Tarot cards.

Sea Nymph

When the broken gourd of the sky
began spilling ash
people thought they could enter cockpits
or airplanes and witness everything.

fly off in a sashay of polite sparks
as if all
that was left in the world to do was just that

except that I myself continued to breathe
and overnight help myself
to cream puffs

Narcissus

Narcissus bloomed by the empty grate
she kicks her boots off in her purest trance
her body is pure

we must not sit by the grate another moment and write poetry
poetry must be outlawed
as much as the blue light lingering
behind a bunch of grapes
in a still life by
Cezanne

and when they filed out of the homeless shelter
it is important to know what bus they are taking and why
and as overhead random birds
cut back on their glossary of terms

Our Ancestors

our ancestors galloped through the snow
with hooves that were clogged with the frozen fire
of too many Indian battles lost

the happenings of each cold day bore witness
that no western pamphlet has described accurately
Buffalo Bill's circus

in Brooklyn housed
the caged spirits of the departed
heroines of the diamond novels

while peopled with tripods
captured the haunted animal look

don't write poetry in the air about what happened
for the horses will fly in suspended motion
and the snow of a thousand winters never melts
will never melt

and the manes of the horses will remain
and the horses will remember nothing of despair

the gentle prodding of Curtis and his camera
the gentle prodding of historians, pathologists, who
muse and keen over the number of unremembered bones
I know the ancient ones will never cease
powdering the hair of memory

Rumi's Breakfast

Who is that person?
sitting across from us
do you trust her/him?
Do you think she's judgmental?
to tell you the truth dogs make better body guards.

Who needs a body guard?
When the blood in my viens is running circles
around me
without my permission

When I say permission
who gave Harvey permission
to circulate his manifesto?

The blood on my hands
is that of the ancients
you expect me to be kind
I've cut off my beard
several times
because I am blind
besides
my scalp was itchy with dandruff
under my turbine

I keep asking
will you let me in your house for breakfast
but I know you don't like anything about the sound of this

only a dog waits at the door
or a coyote
like this.

I've cut off all my hair
and tried to walk gracefully
without announcing my belief: life is never fair
did you just happen to be there?
Did you donate your wig
to breast cancer survivors?

I've lived here in this town all my life
but still I can't claim the doorway of your house as my own
and the threshing floor
for my hair
is littered with the ghosts of fancy dancers

She Told So Many Lies

she told so many lies
about my life

he said
I became

a non-scientifically proven fact of my own non-existence

Companion

I stir my cup of tea at the heart
line cafe
I wait for the sugar to dissolve
If only could break free
Of the enchantment
then the smoke by the river
near a nest of trees would float
higher than my soul would dare
what perfect company I would keep:
zen brush-strokes with great emphasis
birds singing of the great emptiness

Portrait of Jacintha

when I contemplate the moment of Jacintha
I wonder if they'll make shipping charges
I wonder if it'll be an open casket,
It's abysmal to think over the question about whether it will be an
open casket or closed

market research has regularly revealed
people living over eighty
tend to become more holier than thou
every step they take and in their manner of thinking
it's only normal said the contessa

as the flounder's eye revolves in the skull
so does the summer blossoms of the azalea
appear more and more beautiful
in the Sears and Roebucks Catalogue
you can buy miniature and very colorful
Indian headdresses for a 4 year old child
it demonstrates the power of the rosary beads
beaded by the Sioux and the Sioux alone

on the good morning america TV channel last night they
demonstrated the sanctity of the Indian war bonnet and how it
protected the Chieftains from arrows, bullets, and waterproof rain
pellets to represent an Indian war bonnet a scientist complained his x-
wife must've really hated him because when she had sent him the
museum war bonnet it was full, tiny bugs

a traffic cop had to be called in to stop
the altercation between feathers and man eating viruses

Christy Is Always Late

you know how Christy is always late
it's because he's angry
and he has more important things to do
than monitor your mind
and tell you a thing or two

she is still braiding her hair
and it's half past eight
she's still braiding the eye holes of her sneakers
with wispy bits of string

a song bird hops on a single twig
beside a sink that's wrenched from the wall
and tossed on its backside
a magpie lears menacingly
he too is late
he drops two feathers
he knows his fate

sometimes prayer is simply not enough
for prayer has been expended
over too many centuries by saints that collided with their souls
and a visionary the soul is dies to itself and wings from meandering
angels turn granite before their time

Dover Boarding Home

We rented a small room in the Tomahawk Hotel,
A suitable name for a most celebrated musical quartet.
All the while I stayed abroad, I wondered about
The defunct Indian head dresses marveled at
By the masses in the Heard Museum.
Even one stood in a glass case in the living room.

Was the landlord a true art connoisseur?
A Kensington Collector of sorts? Had he ever put
His London home up on the auction block?
How did he come by all these antique works of art?
No one ever asked impertinent questions
About his surreal taste for aesthetics.

Because of pictures of Trobriand Islanders
Formatted in a permissible shade of grey
You'd almost forget to take notice the tasseled cushions
Dangling to one side of the striped faux silk chaise longue.
Because several surreal oil portraits
Of jazz musicians lined the parlor wall,
It seemed they mended trumpets blaring
From the newly painted crimson walls,
Could anyone improve upon such love of art?
Should I go and move to Mount Parnassus
Or instantaneously remove myself to Paris?

The landlord was convinced his boarding home
Not suitable for foundling or orphaned children.
Of course his woman wore the same faded gingham apron
Suitable for all pleasantries on all occasions.

Yet, for all that, Samuel's erratic breakfast repertoire
Continued to stimy her and made her retreat to the kitchen.
Even when the landlords journeyed to Cheltenham's
Literary Festival and then on to Turnbridge Wells.
Nothing quite caught her fancy like Samuels's acting out.

The landlord owned two dogs.
A dog named Pickles not Spot
As well as another pint-sized hound
Named Fractal but certainly not Fritz.
Fractal's back looked like a poster
Pertaining to a non-existent
Clause as to the possible uses of Minimalist Art.
Endorsed Perpetually by Our Lady of Impenetrable Mercy.

Off hours when the local pubs were closed and cloned
In attics of the petulant and the hearing impaired
Darkness caused you to want to meander freely on the goat paths
Among the heather as well travel along the narrow streets of Dover
Of course, this was at a time
When you were young and of a sound mind
That you might meditate on the zeitgeist of particle physics
And upon charming messages embedded
In the Mayan prophecies of the Popol Vuh
As well as the last will and testament
Of the end of the world prophecies
Propagated by Mother Theresa and the miracles
Of Medjugorje.

Near the end of her life,
Mother Theresa, never one to admit she sensed
There was a great god in the porthole of the sky,
Preferred to confide in her biographers
Rather she'd lost all signs of faith

When seeking to restore her energy
With stents instead of much prayed
For metaphors standing in for faith.
Yet, during all of your meandering,
You still wondered why the two dogs
Appear so very fond
Of worrying about the heels
Of derelict rent tenants.
Why bother to bond with members
Belonging to the Bricolage School
When you can have birds nest soup
At the local hangouts of the mandarin school?

But who was Samuel?
While his mother called him Samuel
Perhaps he carried some other name
From way back. His Polish family
May have run out of amateurish rules
Or rites of geneaology. No fool, each day
Samuel went to play in the park
And discussed his near death experience
While his mother wrote down everything
He said in a little dilapidated black notebook.
Samuel, a four year old appeared
To have far memory as advanced
By metaphysical hypnotherapist
Joan Grant. Seemed Samuel
Reincarnated as a miniature Indian chief,
While eating bangers and mash one morning,
Samuel was all too eager to adopt Pickles

The landlord played along
And allowed him to recite
Several songs implying ownership.
Samuel kept repeating: a foreshortened version
Of a sing a long mantra, one chakra long.
My dog, my dog, oh my baby dog

My dog unleashed upon the floor
I will kick his butt for being forlorn
O, I will never be lonely. I will throw a ball for him.
Never give up being kind to my dog.
Never give up on the magic words.
The tricks I can teach him.
In his make-believe poem, Samuel made up his mind.
Most of the other tenants never lacked
For a childhood having been
There done that all along.
Meanwhile the landlord said.
Come sit on my knee, Samuel.

Meanwhile, the landlord would make moan:
It is inexcusable to keep a baby dab chick
Under wraps in a boarding home
For unwed dab chick mothers and elders.
Poor child, up all hours of the night, Samuel is.
True, he will never have a baby brother.
True, check the box, the authorities
Have tied off the ovaries of all the whales.
No wonder we are an endangered species.
Quite often the landlord asked himself:
Should I not turn this sole proprietor's mini hotel
Into a veritable animal shelter?

Samuel cries and cries.
Somehow even in the crisis over ownership
He knows he belongs and does not belong.
Doesn't everyone in the world
Have a special lapdog he/she holds dear?
What is wrong with everyone else
In the world? What is it that I lack? Samuel asks.
Is it true my mother loves me any less

Than hew newly departed husband
And her girlfriend who is always at her side?
Yet still, I love my spirit dog best.
The one dog, the one who goes
And comes and takes walks and wags his tail
And cuts my heart to the quick:
The one I call Mr. Tenderness.
Though I've never heard tell of Elvis
From across the water
In the land of plenty.

The Maid

The Maid went upstairs to procure a dinner for Pickles
How many people here have dogs? Samuel enquired.
Everyone has a dog, Trudy told Samuel
Trudy was the Maid, but she dressed in hip boots
And some tres chique marks and sparks
Jump suits that matched the Victorian wallpaper.

Phillip's wife on the other hand,
Was totally a picture post card wife
She always presented as a comic strip imposter
Here comes Pickles now, said Mary who was Philip's wife.
We have to take him for his daily routine by the sea.
The dog began walking on hind legs
Like a circus dog. We taught him
Every trick he knows both Philip
And Mary said in unison.

Five hundred yards out three scuba divers began searching
For a capsized kayak and for
Wind surfing sail boat, the three scuba
Divers frolicked for a while
Meanwhile Pickles scampered
There there, there's a good watch dog
The Landlord said as he patted Pickles on the head.

Philip always said the dog was his best friend alter ego
And helped him deal with all the inmates
For which he was paid gobs of money
There was Jake, the Russian sailor
There was Mavis the twin sister of Myrtle,

And then the various backpackers from New Zealand and Australia
Who just came for a few days,
And made the place look like a regular motel

In the morning Samuel and his mother carried on
A dialogue fit for the pages of Hamlet
Samuel said I want my sausage,
His mother says my Samuel will not talk back to me
Will not curse me, will not reinvent or revisit childhood
Will not talk back to the landlord
Thought he might wish so to do
Will not have his tea, unless I tell him
I am the one who gave him permission to be born
Not his father who wanted an abortion
Remember, Samuel, to eat all of your egg

One day Samuel was gone, and his mother
Trudy's friend disappeared in a river near the park
Where Myrtle said she was the mother of all children
And refused to travel with Patrick to Ireland
We've all had enough of our Patrick's she said
But when Samuel disappeared
The landlord had his son watched the motel for the weekend
And his son said I'll let you know if anything goes on, but nobody
Knew what the goings on were,

I know I can depend on my son to keep watch
On the beach side motel while I am gone

Sugar Bowl

The last I heard

the first dream consisted
of a silver sugar bowl,
a family heirloom of sorts,
it used to sit right over there on the lazy susan
next to marigolds the color of marmalade and amber

I want to write my grandmother a letter
she used to tell me: we try so hard
to understand her poetry, but we simply can't

grandmother,
it's not worth it,
don't bother
you do enough
for everyone else
but you've left someone out
it's about my daughter

you never tried her picture out
next to my eldest, the one born
to a bloody Englishman,
god forgive him

later in the dream when I looked
at the sugar bowl, I never suspected
it was brimming with sacred ash
ash that came from Louisiana
or the old Ohio or even the Mississippi

oh only say that you'll be mine
and in no other's arms entwine

it's about Indian names all right
a woman run a marathon in pink tights
and a black t-shirt that reads
my-Indian-name-is runs-for-beer

when she spits at my daughter's back
I remember my grandmother's vanity table
don't look back, the past is almost over
flood with unbelievable memories
dead center there is nothing left
to mourn

now I want to return to the dream
six foot under in a tomb enclosure
meant for kings or queens or servants

what's written on the marble slab
in Roman numerals may signify
the monkey god or maybe his cousin
depending on mass consciousness
anything you want

depending on the level of the dreamer
gone to heaven or gone out to lunch
I don't which
I have an astrological hunch
two or eleven can mean
the same thing
in the eyeless midnight of the dream

I am a banner of a dream
draped over my left shoulder

I'm not sure if the feast

of the twelve grandmothers
keeps god alive or not
or whether Creator or Great Spirit
has a bounty on its head

you, my daughter plays an uneasy violin
before you go away I reach for the soap
dish one last time
just fiddling around
is what the news reporter says

because you are different
you have to be the best in town
true, the sheriff always kept
his eagle eye on you

a thousand parchment skins
could never be placed on recall
in pitch and putt games
with the soap dish

who would have thought the sugar bowl
awoke the memory of the children from the past
children who ran so fast
while sugar granules slid underfoot
like coal cinders in winter or like sand in summer heat

if anyone ever imagined of falling down
they knew they could be shot
who knew how to move away
in time for crystal night to take effect
it was all part of history
so the people say

why live in denial

when a Polish gentleman
is arrested in another town
in Ohio but not in Germany
auto-unions could interfere
but is it fair to extradite the clown
perhaps one leaves it up to family

in that way a heart transplant
may
take him
out of tombstone
with great finality

Elevator Shaft Following

I fell down an elevator shaft, and I've carried churches ever since, I used to be in construction. During the war I memorized every single cowboy song in the west, they call it the medieval west where I come from. Now Buffalo Woman, and I have been partners for over fifty years or something and my wife hasn't a clue or anything to do with it. It's just a nice singing arrangement, that's what it is.

Now here's the problem if you know all the names of those songs, I won't quote all of them. I think I recall over 25 songs that are famous. If only people knew how to follow the rules of this church they would know exactly where they stand before god, and then I keep the atmosphere light in this church by singing cowboy songs to make people laugh. It's as if I went to clowning school and never returned.

My buffalo woman, we don't know any of the neighbors, we just possess our congregations one after another, we just process Not proselytize but just let those with parasols take the back row.

We offer prizes some for the children, some for the old people, a little bit of everything. And Buffalo Woman she visited Elvis's birth place. She collects Elvis memorabilia and wears little runic charm bracelets. Sometimes we have massaging ceremonies that's where it gets a little cold in a little black tent. The molding ceremonies are so exciting Henry James wrote about them in his early works.

Melon

Ms. Pritchet's sociology class took place in the garden at four o clock in the afternoon. People from the four corners came in with their hiking boots, and took out their manuscripts, describing how the rest of the world had apple dumplings for breakfast. The sociology teacher, Ms. Pritchet took out melons. Get a load of this, she said. Everyone spit out the pits in a straight line. Why had she called this a safe haven? Everyone got A on the sociology course even Maeve and Denise who never spoke in class.

Coda

When the motor making light will have finished with the dark, you and I, shall remain as ashen leaves in a goat park whose electric wire fence has long ago failed. Everyone who has been asked to grow their own vegetables didn't listen nor when the airplanes flew into buildings they forgot Grandmother's prayer for healing. She'd had the dream in nineteen seventy three, she told everyone about the dream and no one listened, but she's still praying, and papaya seeds are still planted until eternity chimed and end of time, timeless time. It's no more buddy do you happen to have a dime?—it's rather if only you would have come to Ireland, and watched it be pulled by Cuchulainn's legions you would've known in time why people in fur line boots salute to Brown Bear, who has patience enough to wait for the salmon leaping from the falls. Otherwise you might accuse the people of some wayward tribe as hibernating way passed time.

Old Age

You're looking great
they said to Myrtle and yet she was becoming older by the day
her small vase from the Ming dynasty
stood cracked on the mantle in the parlor

she took one or two tablets a day
and settled and settled in her chair like a noiseless spider
that had constructed lattices
flung in the midnight air

the petulant lip droops
the hands grow weary of their own intelligence
she toasts a non-existent relative
and smoothes the freakish white streaks in her hair
she is miserly with kindness
she is compassionate in the way of the west wind

in a clearer picture than this
she would've dissolved the window frame all together
and noticed how spotless the shelves of snow in winter weather
and marked the dissolving coyote's laughter

Conversion

Myrtle joins the bible thumpers. I don't want to belong to any church, I just want to belongs to one that leaves me time that tells me stories. I have then all enthralled in the Baptist church so I stay there. I tell them stories of my trips with Patrick to Tibet, to Ireland, and to Florida. And they believe every story because Baptists believe every word that is written in a book, about lives, and truths. I live between the life of life, and lies about the truth, I live between two continents, and am ruthlessly amiable.

I live between what it takes to talk to Patrick, and the church parishioners I channel the spirits of unborn children. Right over there, there is a funeral mound for all the children aborted by the British during the war who saved the German parachute jumpers. There's a little mound of them right over there, I'm glad my father was a Quaker I wouldn't dare, he never knew what I would think during the war. He said now you're up for Quaker loss, now what I was getting to is that: now you're up against it. Funny odd and comical thing, he never knew how many children were aborted in the mound all about the bad hill, we call it Elephant Hill to cover for all our losses and we leave little flowers by the unlettered graves.

Yes I used to play with the church until they kicked me out for having an affair with the young organist Why did they call it Unitary, there's no Unity at all. They have to import a new minister almost every week from different states, from different shires, from different counties. Did I tell you the pulpit is unstable in the church the only thing stable is my heart. For ,in my heart, I know I channel nothing but angels, and my golden hair is an asset even if I do say so myself. Every note I play is ecologically molded and marked and set to a specific sound that will echo with mother earth. And if I do have an affair with the odd parishioner, or two so what, friends, who really cares? It's good for their souls because I've been an angelic from the get go. Since I saw you last, I've taken three courses in psychology: Eco-psychology, church law and finance. I used to have a library detailing all of my ancient appearances: that was when my hair was dyed black, and I was confused about who I truly was. Now I paint my nails with fairy gloss, and every note I play reaches from here to somewhere to where to where.

From Dover to Edinburgh you'll never catch me playing a note of jazz. We had a jazz pianist in our church just once, he didn't last long, his notes failed to harmonize with my angelic heart, they don't call me Angelica for nothing. When I finish my cooking class, and open my bakery called Angel bread then people will know who I am as if they could ever forget. In Borneo we should grow nothing but cocoanut trees.

Everyone knows I don't know where the world ends. Then boundary of reason is extraterrestrial and so anything goes. Even if the wave comes, the deluge is still only in the realm of the unknown. Without large doses of yak butter, everyone will be destined to lose his/her way in the universal path of whatever leads to disaster.

Truth Serum

nobody is in charge of anybody else
the sherif has absconded with the camera
the cherry tree has absconded with the truth

the broom used in the museum
that houses antiques has dropped
several whiskers

it's very strange but nobody
is in charge or anything

Memory of a Dead Sparrow

Don't wash your dirty linen in the park
In all the secret places of the heart, let the fire burn itself out
It is I am innocence who would ask what is with this poem?
Also know this the sparrow lives in a dark underbrush,
In a dark place where no one knows him
He is anonymous as the lost blood
Of other winters. You figure that one out.
The ghost of Aunt Martha time does not matter here.
If in s manner of minutes a small sparrow falls earthward
In time-honored rumors of minutes assail him with the truth
No one knows exactly how many angels confess
Their jiggory-pokery on the head of a pin.
If at night, when on skid row, thieves begin their miracles
It makes you think of what you did before you dropped the body.
Among wind-driven rooms of stone castles and palaces
No one knows what you have gone through
Nor do they want to know, really they don't
How did the sparrow figure out
The end of the world really near at hand?
Grief-stricken, did his relatives tell him
Or some other infinite source he missed
Nor did anyone ever understand
What needed to be understood
As fully as it was deemed it should.

In a matter of minutes when a small sparrow falls earthward
Who when felled unexpectedly, who sheds a tear
In the choir stalls unexpectedly no one makes amend
After the funeral is ended and everyone goes forth in peace
Or maybe they don't remember any details about the legacy

Of that person's august life. At my mother's funerals
My father told me stay by my side don't say a word
Momma is not going to buy you a mocking bird in fact
She won't leave you a single necklace or any jewels
To bedeck your miserable body with since you
Gave up dancing you're so out of shape it's not funny
Well dad if you did not worship the family dog
More than me and take care of her more carefully
What happened would never have happened to me
Or to you for that matter in fact you almost gave your life
For your son and what did he care did he end up
Loving you all the same or did he suddenly
Take up the palette a ghost of time's restless
Minutes who will save you really no one will
There is really no one like you and you know it
Whatever happens everyone will know it
Before it ever happens anyway people are becoming
So psychic these days they scarcely know how to
Complete a memory map of the entire world
Or complete washing their dirty linen in public

And become a first rate artist?
Dad all you have to do is pick up the phone
And call me but instead you want to suffer
And act as if it is still 1943 and I am still at home
With mum and you don't even want to get to know me
Or you didn't have the time in a strange way I still love you
Yes I do dad

Grief-stricken did he know how near the end he was or not
Perhaps a sparrow floats out to see as listless as a mother
Who asks that all the furniture be moved from her room
And that her bed be put by an open window in the living room
Where all can catch a glimpse of her at the last minutes
Of her incarnation? Do you think the sparrow
Believes in anything but the supreme goddess
Who puts before you the beginning and end of sewing sessions,

Coffee klatsches movie get-togethers or having tennis lessons
Or bowling matches before the end is near?
How entertain the ghosts of wayward stations
How maintain your composure and your proper
His multiple timelines are so all encompassing
He doesn't have to reincarnate alone
When the thunderous applause happens
Always a lightening flash fails and misses its mark completely
Once again you are alone
And anything that happens fails to strike home.

How many artists leave their easels in the park?
Suddenly everyone is willing to blurt out the evening new
The impudent speaks unwisely about the wise
And the wise make mistakes and grapple with the truth
Even so you are branded a liar even if you are truthful
And wander around the hedgerow with a bible
Or a blank piece of paper. A pen? Something must be
Going on knitting needles continue knitting
Even after dark why should I have to defend myself to you?
A skylark knows better how to jump off a roof
Or into a swimming pool some kind of shenanigans
The archer misses the bull's eye all the time.
What of it?

How many artists leave their easels in the park?
Suddenly everyone is willing to blurt out the truth
The stock market crash as well as Mother Shipton's Prophecy
Are totally out of date. Nostradamus?
Oh everyone has had enough of him.
The channel is broken that was once open.
So what if everyone stores data in computers
And decides to leave it all behind.
The diner the little walks to the station
The price of eggs too much to comment upon
They will shut down all the super-markets
After the grand slam tennis final

Suddenly the veins in your hands have grown
Almost unrecognizable and your voice is lowered almost in a whisper
And nothing sounds the same
The words recited are a little under sung
By the multitude who have to listen to your fol de rol
Oh, but, come on, my dear, don't go spoiling your life work
Come on in out of the rain before the song begins again.

Know when to come in out of the rain my dear
Know which side of the toast is buttered
It just a matter of time when everyone will be afraid
And they won't know where to move to
Why spoil the makings of your life work?
Come now come along inside bring your umbrella inside
Why not volunteer at a prison?
By Monday or Tuesday fellow workers
Or colleagues begin their wisecracks about inclement weather
The price of gimcrackers eggs dog walkers
Begin their alphabets of city-streets
Book-seller open their awnings
Once again everyone realizes life is sweet
Among the nomadic artists.
Nothing so reprehensible as the life of the damned
Or the man that runs a stoplight on a city street
Forewarned without warning
I wonder how many parishioners are content
Have their attended church even once
Before the new minister came
You know the one who features the choirmaster
And speaks out of both sides of his mouth
The cost of canvases and colored chalks are out of sight

The price of birth baths impossible to decipher
Today haven't you discerned what happens to everyone
When each person and his brother vies with one another
To do more than his share at what cost to mother earth
And to the health of rivers

When worker drops his body hasn't it become quite clear
Who is adept at giving dalliance to time-honored truths?
The grand slam poetry contest is on once again
No matter that it takers beer to even begin the round
Is it any wonder like it or not
Such soul painting conceived in madness
Of minarets and mosques often find their way
To the auction block where the artists are tied for first place?
Is it any wonder then faithfully rendered
In the Marketplace anything is up for grabs?

Each soulful rendition of a painting
Sighing men wipe each other's eye
As time demands to know who is adept
At such bitter dalliance with time shared
And god given truths spawns a lesser truth
Than what can be countered with what is
Tied for first place at the auction block?
This happens not out of ignorance

But rather in a momentary embrace
Of a blameless dance of truth and justice
A momentary dance blames and innocent
In the first instance at first almost everyone looks in denial
Innocent or involved with other things
Self-absorbed but I am innocent of any wrong doing
What are you doing?
Someone suspects no one could be innocent

Of some kind of wrongdoing.
Under duress, is that true you succumbed to the temptation
Of how many confessions heard an unheard?
Tweezers can uproot the last whisker of a beard
And in the end hair-splitting decisions
Are those that are made at births, weddings, wakes, and in between
When nothing is really going on, today don't you know
You must puzzle over the memory of ministering angels?

Books by Elizabeth Martina Bishop
All books available through Amazon.com

Irish Tinkers

(Written under pseudonym Martina O' Fearadhaigh) with photographs by Janine Wiedel

The origin of the Irish Tinkers and of their secret language, shelta, has long been the subject of fierce controversy amongst historians. Some say the were forced into an itinerant existence by the social and economic upheavals of the 17th century; others that they are descendants of a pre-Celtic class of skilled metal workers and others that they are the remnants of dispossessed nobility. But whatever their origins the Irish Tinkers are now threatened on all sides. This book is a permanent record of this curiously resilient people made while there is still time. The moving photographs together with the transcribed tape-recordings which show the tinkers' extraordinary eloquence as they talk about their lives, reveal the anguish of a people in transition; nostalgia for 'the old days' and uncertainty about the future.

ISBN-10: 0312436270 • ISBN-13: 978-0312436278.

Feathers in the Wind

Feathers in the Wind represents a compilation of interrelated themes reflected in indigenous inspired portraits, both lyric and pastoral. It evidences the author's deep connection to the mystical aspects of nature and her continuing dedication to the traditional craft of poetry.

ISBN-13: 978-1461030874
ISBN-10: 1461030870 • $9.95

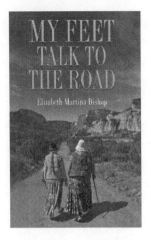

My Feet
Talk to the Road

Traveller culture projects masks involving multiple scenarios. The way of the road may never disappear. The way of the settled folk continues to change. With the disappearance of many itinerant crafts today is born a new integration honoring the old crafts. These days, we can nevertheless appreciate time-honored traditions that invite readers to enter a transcendent dream time. Such an invitation is always present for those who risk a continuous pilgrimage. That is the fearless way of the traveling people.

ISBN-13: 978-1461129646 • ISBN-10: 1461129648 • $14.95

Canary Portals

Canaries have symbolized the healing properties of the sun. Many folk cultures feature the canary as a Rosicrucian dream image showing the canary hovering above a rose. In this narrative poem the canary operates as a fixture, a landmark, leading the dreamer in a journey celebrating life, birth and death.

ISBN-13: 978-1463551179
ISBN-10: 1463551177 • $9.95

Soulmate in a Kayak

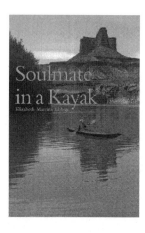

Vignette 1: Soulmate in a Kayak
This section depicts a surreal treatment of a fictitious want ad and the fallout thereof.

Vignette 2: Dervish in a Kiosk
The poems deconstruct the want ad.

Vignette 3: Reinventing Atlantis
Ishti poses questions for those living in so-called civilized society: how can we honor what we don't know we have lost.

Vignette 4: The Green Knight
A pseudo medieval melodrama involving a lovelorn swain who suffers and endures the worst case scenario in a love tryst gone wrong.

ISBN-13: 978-1461154921 • ISBN-10: 1461154928 • $19.95

Leaping into the Unknown

A woman reflects on the meaning of life and turns the sheepfold into a museum, a sunken garden, and a palimpsest of poetry and art.

ISBN-13: 978-1463741334
ISBN-10: 1463741332 • $19.95

Malvinia's Wedding

A folkloric portrait of a woman waiting by various gates for her beloved who may never arrive.

The locations depicted in the text are considered in a visionary and fictional manner.

Part dream, part reverie the quilt of stories supports tribal voices heard in the region of Moorish Spain.

ISBN-13: 978-1475161427 • ISBN-10: 1475161425 • $19.95

The Wedding Will Not Take Place

This poetic novel promises an occasion for celebration and ceremony. Meanwhile, the ritual of ceremony exists only within the mind of the celebrants who are on the point of undertaking a long journey.

This novel promises an ambitious time line involving the completion of a journey. However, no actual ritual of ceremony is actually performed. Instead, the act of writing is seen as a self-redemptive and self-revelatory journey occasioning a spiritual awakening. In the spirit of "Waiting for Godot," celebrants and attendants engage in long journeys of pilgrimage, ultimately leading them towards an inner heart-centered labyrinth. A novel approach to writing a novel without an apparent ending or beginning, words in themselves represent an exploration of the psyches of those who would prepare for a centered afterlife of joy and renunciation.

ISBN-13: 978-1475161205 • ISBN-10: 1475161204 • $18.95

Wind Rushing Through a Nest of Stars

A delectable award-winning study of poetry that will arouse the sleeping palette of connoisseurs.
A wine-tasting array of poetry that shifts our focus to environmental causes. Poems with emotional clout bring us to a deeper sense of awareness. We awake from our sleep with poetry and well crafted poems singing before we take on the day.

ISBN-13: 978-1475182835 • ISBN-10: 147518283X • $14.95

Your Grandmother Knew How To Read Cards

From time immemorial, grandmothers have been in the know about the occult arts.
They also know how to read palms.
Some of them even write poetry that will make you laugh.

ISBN-13: 978-1479132232
ISBN-10: 1479132233 • $ 9.95

101

Stonehenge Blues Vol. 1

A mysterious and poignant exploration of poetic memoir to deepen an awareness of who we are and where we are headed. In days of uncertainty we find our footing. We find poetry in an urban coming of age story. How does one interpret life events that seem in old age to have a dream-like quality? In any event it is up to each individual to transmute and transform seemingly meaningless events. Eventually, we find out we are wordsmiths who must take the time to witness hidden worlds. In that way, the art of becoming becomes an art form. We discover who we were all along: pilgrims and solitary seers.

ISBN-13: 978-1479294268 • ISBN-10: 1479294268 • $9.95

Stonehenge Blues Vol. 2

Stonehenge Blues represents the continued journey into the life cycle of birth, marriage, and death. When bohemian-minded poets get together, they have unique ways of summoning forth the wilderness of heart songs. Their world is ever expanding, one which embraces life's teaching moments. That perspective ultimately leads to meditation in the wise solitude of old age. You may want to look at such moments of great passionate intensity with a sense of humorous non-attachment.

ISBN-13: 978-1479294329 • ISBN-10: 1479294322 • $9.95

Carillon Players and Night Watchmen

These poems celebrate an abandoned culture of relationship and an industry based on handcrafts. A cross between the melancholia of a lost way of life and contemporary media driven culture. Between the old world of wandering minstrels, Indian warriors, and a new world in which technology is often the new poetry.

ISBN-13: 978-1480271425 • ISBN-10: 148027142X • $9.95

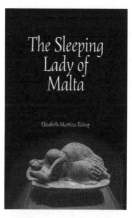

The Sleeping Lady of Malta

An archeological gem, The Sleeping Lady of Malta explores relationship between human, animal and nature and the mystery that no one single poem can evoke.

Native American images predominate because they are cloaked with formidable shadows. This collection offers a credo as to why I write poetry. To experience banner moments of consciousness wherein aesthetics and a love of word smithing is born. The quest for self-knowledge and self-revelation takes nature as its meditation.

ISBN-13: 978-1481946421 • ISBN-10: 1481946420 • $9.95

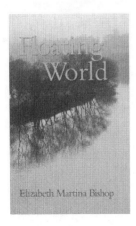

Floating World

Poetic excursions and aesthetic
exercises that demonstrate
the power of the word.
The journey readers take will
show them unique pathways through
often oblique patterns and designs.
Experimental in nature,
these poems push the envelope
of time and space and
express gratitude for the spiritual.

ISBN-13: 978-1482613186 • ISBN-10: 1482613182 • $9.95

And Then I Heard
Them Singing

For poets, the culture of every day life
involves engagement and interaction implicit
in her ongoing conversation.
A conversation with creatures of the natural
world.
These poems offer whimsical and often
comical glimpses into old age, thoughts about
the afterlife, and the daily karma of survival.

ISBN-13: 978-1482762853 • ISBN-10: 1482762854 • $9.95

Round House Dances

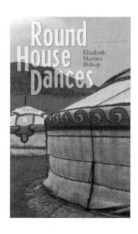

Round House Dances gifts readers with glimpses into the worlds of the bee shaman, views of the natural world in Ireland and in Boulder, as well as additional encounters with teachers and students.

Everyday experiences surrender readers with poetic vignettes, philosophical, scintillating, meditative, and reflective.

A must read for those who seek heart-centered poetry.

ISBN-13: 978-1482763331 • ISBN-10: 1482763338 • $9.99

The Mud Palace of Aberdeen

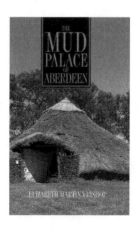

Here are cogent poems that ask questions. Questions that cannot necessarily be answered.
Or poetic explorations of parallel worlds. Explorations into unknown and uncharted territory. A whirlwind tour of Native American shamanism. Or just plain shamanism.

The price of being a poet is to create unexplained patchwork quilts in response to the more mysterious aspects of the world around us.
Come and enjoy and savor the poetic experience as rich as a good cup of coffee savored in the universal cafe, scintillating, meditative, and reflective.

ISBN-13: 978-1484926918 • ISBN-10: 1484926919 • $9.95

Made in the USA
Charleston, SC
25 June 2013